# TO THE TEACHER

FAR OUT STORY STARTERS can help your students strengthen their language arts capabilities through the use of their imagination. The characters are charming creatures from outer space. Your students look at the illustrations, read the story starters, and help to complete the adventures by answering the "questions to think about" as well as other questions they might consider themselves. They then write their own endings for the stories.

The material has been tested with children from kindergarten through fifth grade. The material had high interest appeal but limited written use at the kindergarten and first grade levels. Teachers, aides, or cross age tutors had to read the stories aloud and students then dictated simplified story endings to them. Older students, who read the stories themselves, created lengthier and more complex endings. All the students enjoyed the stories and the illustrations.

Accompanying each illustration is a narrative that sets the stage, introduces a cast of characters, and outlines the beginning of a plot. Questions provide **hints** for the student who sometimes says, "I don't know what to write about." It should be stressed that they are "thought provokers" rather than to be used by the student to help determine the outcome of the story.

Each story starter launches the young writer on a space flight of imagination and a writing exercise in which there are no wrong answers. Show your appreciation for every imaginative detail provided by the student.

## How to Use These Story Starters

These story starters can be used effectively in a variety of ways. Choose the way that best meets the needs of your students. Here are some alternatives:

1. Distribute duplicated story starters and illustrations, along with writing paper, during the regular reading or language arts period. Read the story aloud, ask an aide to do it or have the students read to themselves. Hold a discussion to encourage imaginative suggestions and call attention to any unfamiliar words. Ask the students to complete each story ending. If you have distributed writing paper, the students can begin to write immediately while their ideas are still fresh. When they have finished, invite the students to share their stories aloud.

2. It is suggested that the material be read to those students who are reading at second grade level or below. Each of these students can dictate a story ending into a tape recorder or to an aide, who writes or types it. They may each copy the story ending after the aide has transcribed each person's dictation.

3. The material may also be sent home with a note as to best use of parent/student involvement.

4. The pages in this book can be pasted on cardboard, laminated, and placed in a learning center or at an activities table. The student can then be encouraged to write and draw other stories as supplementary activities.

5. You may want to extend the activity beyond story completion. For example, you might ask students to write a story about **themselves** and the creatures in the picture. Students may color the pictures while they think about stories they will write and/or illustrate.

---

### MAKE YOUR OWN MASTERS
This book is perforated so that each sheet may be easily removed. Spirit Duplicating Masters (dittos) may be made via the thermofax process. Multi-copy the activities and awards for student use and to help you individualize in the classroom.

---

Note to Teachers:
You can get these same space characters in Full Color as 11" x 16" posters when ordering ENCOUNTERING NUMBERS (EN 74003) from your school supply dealer.

Carol L. King - Author
Patricia M. Horton - Editor
Rob Browne - Artist

FAR OUT STORY STARTERS EN75207RR  © 1979, ENRICH, INC., Sunnyvale, CA 94086   Printed in U.S.A.

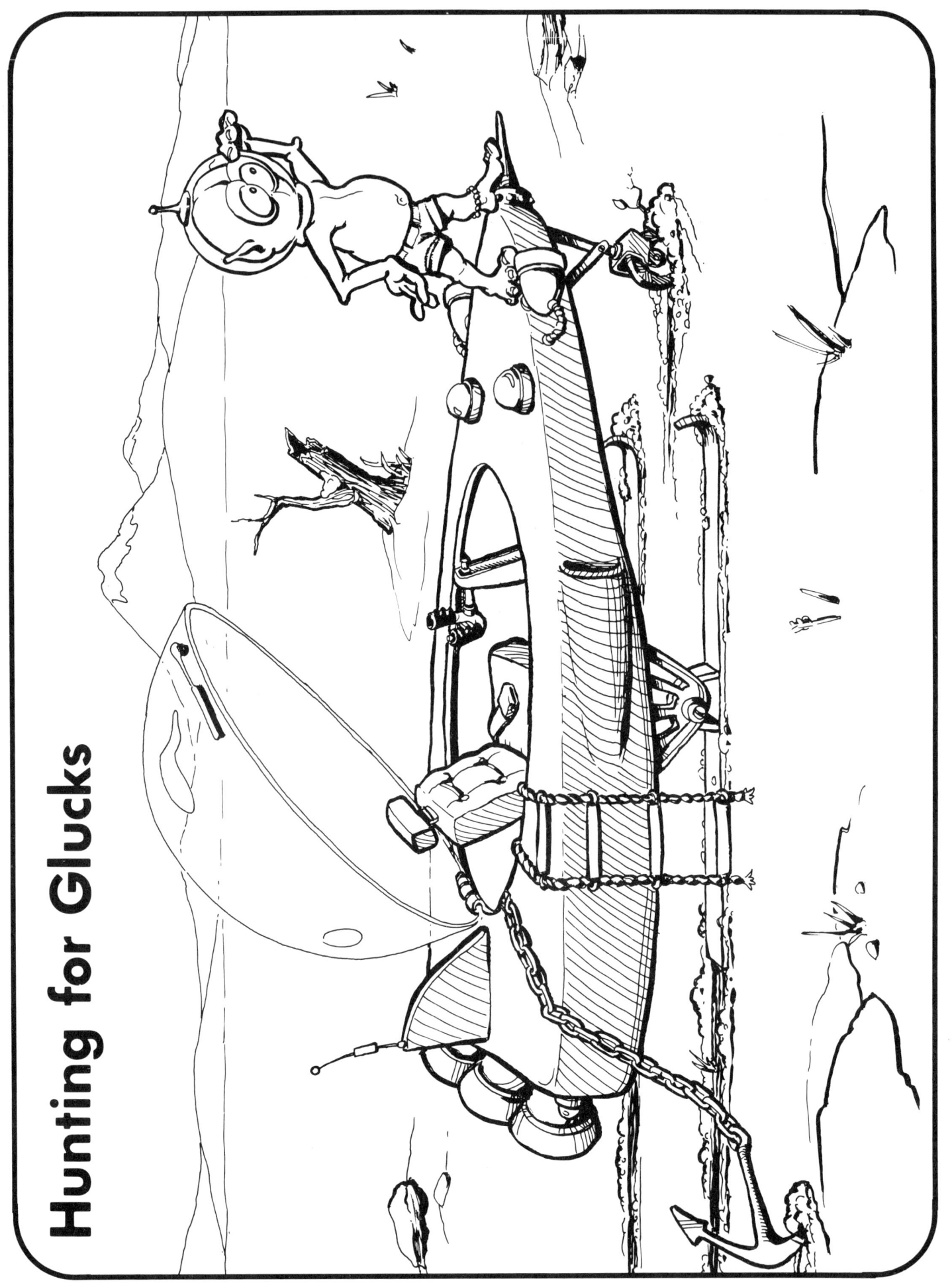

# Hunting for Glucks

# Hunting for Glucks

Barbara and Jean saw something drop down from the sky. "It's a space ship!" cried Barbara.

"A toy space ship," Jean said. The ship was about the size of a skateboard.

"No, it's not a toy," the space man answered. "It's a real space ship from a very small planet. My name is Sampebblewitz. But you can call me Sam." Sam was a tiny blue creature, only one foot tall.

"I'm a scientist," Sam said. "I came to earth to study the gluck. I want to take some glucks back to my planet."

"What is a gluck?" Barbara asked.

"I don't know your name for the gluck," Sam said. "It is an animal with eight legs. Most glucks are black or brown. You have millions of glucks here on earth."

"We'd better find him some glucks so he can take them back to his planet," said Jean.

**Questions to Think About . . .**

How will Barbara and Jean find out what a gluck is? What will happen while they are hunting for glucks? How will the story end?

FAR OUT STORY STARTERS   EN75207   © 1979, ENRICH, INC., Sunnyvale, CA 94086

# The Lost Space Ship

Zig and Zag are people from outer space. They wanted to fly to the moon. But they got lost and landed on Earth. They landed near a park in town. They saw that their space ship was broken. Zig and Zag needed help to fix their ship.

"Where are we?" asked Zig.

Zag looked around. She saw a flower. "There are green things here," she said. "We must be on Earth."

"Good," said Zig. "There are no people on the moon. But there are many people on Earth. They will help us fix our ship."

Zig and Zag did not know what Earth people looked like.

A snake came near the space ship. Zig and Zag saw the snake move.

"Hello, sir," Zig said to the snake. "We are glad to see you. We need help to fix our ship. Can you help us?"

The snake did not answer.

Next a cat came along. The cat stopped to look at Zig and Zag.

"Hello, sir," Zag said to the cat. "We are glad to see you. We need help to fix our ship. Can you help us?"

But the cat did not answer.

Zig and Zag could hear singing, barking, and sounds of playing. Were there people nearby who could help them?

## Questions to Think About . . .

Will Zig and Zag be brave enough to leave their space ship? Will they find help to fix their space ship? How will the story end?

FAR OUT STORY STARTERS   EN75207   © 1979, ENRICH, INC., Sunnyvale, CA 94086

# The Space Ship from Splott

Far away, just north of nowhere, there is a planet named Splott. The people there are called Splottniks.

The air around Splott is not the same as the air here on Earth. If you had to breathe the air on Splott, you would begin to grow taller. But when Splottniks breathe Earth air, they shrink.

Three Splottniks landed on Earth. They opened the door and stepped out of their ship. They began to grow smaller and smaller.

"We're shrinking!" cried their leader. "My clothes are too big!"

One Splottnik fell off the ship. He was too small to get back on. The others tried to think of a way to help.

"We have to act fast!" the leader said. "If we stay here much longer, I'll be too little to fly the ship! We must get back to Splott. Then we'll all grow big again."

The leader tried to think of a way to stop growing smaller. He looked around for something to use as a ladder. He had to get the third Splottnik back on the ship.

## Questions to Think About . . .

How will the Splottniks stop growing smaller? How will the third Splottnik get back on the ship? How will the story end?

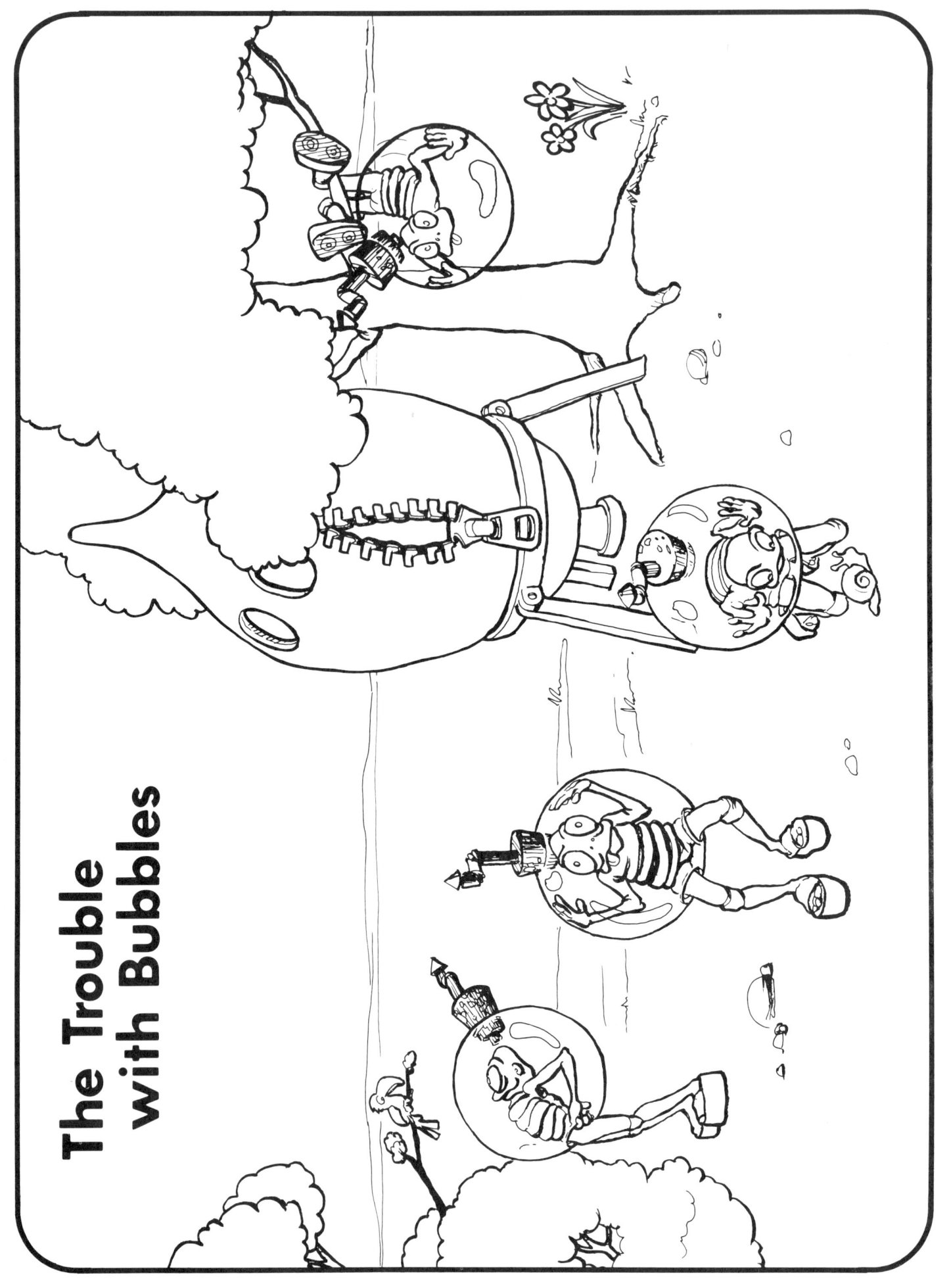

# The Trouble with Bubbles

Maria had a funny dream about a space ship with a zipper on one side.

The space ship landed, and the zipper opened. Four bubbles floated out. One bubble floated into a tree. The other bubbles landed at Maria's feet.

Maria saw a tiny man in each bubble. A little man with big sad eyes spoke to Maria.

"My name is Aard," he said. "I need your help. A wicked witch has cast a spell on us. She made us wear these bubbles. We want to get out of them."

"Why don't you break them?" Maria asked.

"We can't," Aard answered. "That is part of the witch's spell."

"I wish I could help you," said Maria, in her dream. "It must be hard to live in a bubble. If you're not careful, you might float away."

"We have been flying from planet to planet," Aard said. "We are looking for the only creature who can break the bubbles."

"Is it a person or a thing?" Maria asked.

## Questions to Think About . . .

Who is the only creature who can break the bubbles? How will Maria be able to help find the creature to break the spell? How will Maria's dream end?

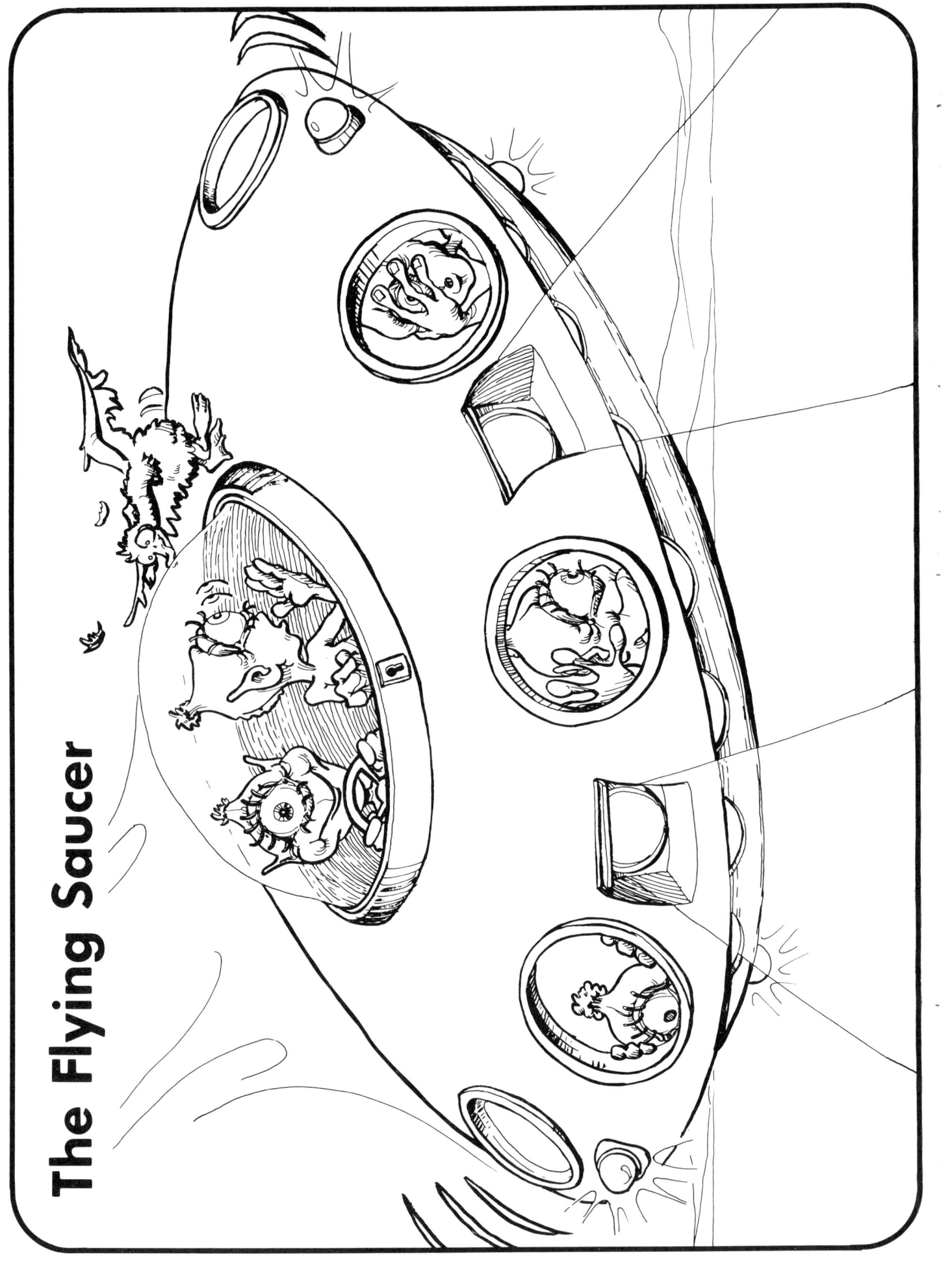

# The Flying Saucer

Scruffy was a bird who told lies. The other birds knew that Scruffy told lies. But they did not know why.

Scruffy thought, "a bird's life is dull." The birds looked for food all day. At night they went to sleep in a tree.

So Scruffy made up stories to tell his friends. The other birds knew his stories were not true. No one believed his stories.

One day Scruffy flew far away from his friends. He saw a round ship sailing in the sky. He flew close to the ship to get a better look.

Scruffy could not believe his eyes! The ship was a flying saucer. Later, he told his friends what he had seen.

"Today I saw a flying saucer," Scruffy said.

The other birds began to laugh.

"It's true," Scruffy said. "I saw a flying saucer. There were five funny men in it."

"What was funny about them?" the other birds asked.

"Each man had only one eye," Scruffy said. "Each had just one big eye in the middle of his face."

The other birds laughed again. "Ha, ha, ha! A one-eyed man! Who could believe a story like that?"

Scruffy felt very bad. He wanted the other birds to believe him.

## Questions to Think About . . .

How will Scruffy make the other birds believe his story? What else will he say that he saw the men in the flying saucer doing? How will the story end?

FAR OUT STORY STARTERS   EN75207   © 1979, ENRICH, INC., Sunnyvale, CA 94086

# Diving for Gold

The Frogmen live on a planet named Squish. They came to Earth to find gold. Frogmen can swim under water and dive all the way to the bottom of the sea.

One dark night, a ship hit some rocks near the shore and sank. It had been carrying gold. No one could reach the gold because of the big rocks in the sea. And there were no roads to the sea.

The Frogmen went by air. They planned to dive into the water from a space ship.

Because they had never dived from a space ship before, they jumped too soon and landed in an old dead tree.

CRACK, CRACK, CRACK! Sounds were coming from the tree. The old wood was beginning to break. The Frogmen had to think fast. What would happen if they jumped from the tree? Would they reach the water? Or would they hit the land?

## Questions to Think About . . .

Will the Frogmen jump out of the tree and land in the water? If they find any gold, how will they carry it away? How will the story end?

FAR OUT STORY STARTERS  EN75207  © 1979, ENRICH, INC., Sunnyvale, CA 94086

# Christmas in July

Santa's elves had a secret. They were building a space ship. But Santa did not know about their ship.

The elves wanted to fly around the world on Christmas eve. They wanted to help Santa give toys to boys and girls.

One day in July, Santa found the space ship.

"What is this funny thing?" he asked.

The elves had to tell him their secret.

"Ho, ho, ho!" Santa said. "That ship will never fly! Besides, you can't make the trip on Christmas eve. You are too little. You could not carry a big bag of toys."

"We will help each other," the elves said.

"No, no, no," said Santa. "You are too little. You could not even slide down the chimneys. They are too tall for you."

That night the elves talked it over. They were sure their ship would fly. They wanted to test it and try out the chimneys.

"Santa is asleep," the elves said. "Let's show Santa we're not too little to make the trip."

Seven elves got into the ship and took off. They flew to your town. They landed on your roof.

## Questions to Think About . . .

Will they slide down your chimney? What will Santa say about their trip? How will the story end?

FAR OUT STORY STARTERS   EN75207   © 1979, ENRICH, INC., Sunnyvale, CA 94086

# No Place to Swim

FAR OUT STORY STARTERS   EN75207   © 1979, ENRICH, INC., Sunnyvale, CA 94086

# No Place to Swim

On a planet called Tumkin, there is no place to swim. Tumkin has very little water. All the water is in deep holes, called wells, and is used for drinking, bathing, and cooking.

The children on Tumkin have studied about Earth. They know that we have lakes, rivers, and oceans but they have never seen a beach. Eight children from Tumkin flew to Earth for a picnic and a swim at the beach. They landed in your back yard by mistake!

If you went to the window to smell the pie your mother baked, you might see eight funny little fellows trying to have a picnic. You could see that they don't know much about picnics because they did not bring any food.

One little fellow might be trying to get your mother's pie.

"Stop!" you would say. "You can't have all that pie!"

But the children from Tumkin do not speak English. The little fellow would answer, "Glup kiddy blug blug."

## Questions to Think About . . .

How will you talk to the space children? Will you show them how to have a picnic and have fun swimming? Will it be a real picnic — or a funny picnic? How will the story end?

FAR OUT STORY STARTERS    EN75207    © 1979, ENRICH, INC., Sunnyvale, CA 94086

# The Animals on Muzz

FAR OUT STORY STARTERS   EN75207   © 1979, ENRICH, INC., Sunnyvale, CA 94086

# The Animals on Muzz

Two scientists flew to a planet called Muzz. From the air, they could see some green plants.

"Today is a big day for science," said Dr. Logan. "Now we know there is life on Muzz."

"At least we know that plants can live on Muzz," said Dr. Garcia. "Let's find out if there are any animals."

They landed their space ship and began to look around. They saw some little animals playing beside a stream. No one had ever seen such animals before. Dr. Garcia called the animals "Muzzies."

"Let's catch some Muzzies," Dr. Logan said. "We can take them back to Earth."

"I think we should leave them alone," said Dr. Garcia. "We don't know how to take care of them. We don't even know what they eat. Without good care, the Muzzies might die."

"But this is our chance to be famous," Dr. Logan answered. Many people will see the Muzzies on TV."

"But maybe they're not animals," said Dr. Garcia. "Maybe they're people, who think and talk like we do. I think we should take pictures of them, then leave them alone."

## Question to Think About . . .

What do you think they will do about the Muzzies? What will the scientists find out about the Muzzies? How will the story end?

# Washing a Rocket

FAR OUT STORY STARTERS  EN75207  © 1979, ENRICH, INC., Sunnyvale, CA 94086

# Washing a Rocket

The Fidgets wash cars every Saturday morning. "Just call us on Friday," they say. "On Saturday, we will come and wash your car."

One Friday they got a call from the school. "Can you wash a school bus?"

"Yes, we can," said the Fidgets.

The next week they washed a small airplane. The Fidgets were very happy about their work. "We can wash anything," they said.

But the very next week the Fidgets had to wash a rocket! The rocket was 30 feet tall. It was as tall as a big building.

On Saturday, the Fidgets began to wash the rocket. They had a mop, a broom and three buckets. They had soap and rags. They had a ladder, but it was too short. The Fidgets could not reach the top of the rocket.

"We need help," the Fidgets said. "Who will help us wash the top of the rocket? Who has a ladder that is 30 feet tall?"

## Questions to Think About . . .

How will the Fidgets reach the top of the rocket? Will they try to wash anything that is bigger than a rocket? How will the story end?

FAR OUT STORY STARTERS   EN75207   © 1979, ENRICH, INC., Sunnyvale, CA 94086

(Note: Please fill in the date, student's name and the subject being studied.)

Date _____

Signed _____

This is to certify that _____

is moving right along in _____.

Date _____

Signed _____

THERE'S JUST NO COMPARISON!

This is to certify that you can't hold a candle to _____

when it comes to _____.

# CERTIFICATE OF ACHIEVEMENT

Strike up the band

for _____

who is doing excellent work in

_____.

Signed _____ Date _____

---

# AWARD OF EXCELLENCE

This award goes to _____
for doing beautiful work in

_____.

Signed _____ Date _____

# ASK YOUR LOCAL SCHOOL SUPPLY DEALER FOR THE GOOD IDEA BOOKS!

## DUPLICATING MASTER BOOKS

GREAT, someone has finally recognized how a teacher really teaches. Now you can quickly and easily provide your students with contemporary, motivational worksheets that are fun to use. Basic skills and concepts are stressed. Limited teacher involvement required.
- 20 pp • 8½" x 11" • Teacher's guide • Curriculum related objectives
- Fun art themes • $4.50

**Math**
| | |
|---|---|
| Monster Addition (Gr. 1-3) | EN75301 |
| Monster Subtraction (Gr. 1-3) | EN75302 |
| Monster Multiplication (Gr. 3-5) | EN75303 |
| Monster Division (Gr. 3-5) | EN75304 |

**Reading/Language Arts**
| | |
|---|---|
| Visual Perception (Gr. K-3) | EN75201 |
| Time To Rhyme (Gr. K-3) | EN75202 |
| Beginning Consonants (Gr. K-3) | EN75203 |
| Understanding Consonants (Gr. 1-3) | EN75204 |
| Short and Long Vowels (Gr. 1-3) | EN75205 |
| Alphabetizing Activities (Gr. 1-4) | EN75206 |
| Far Out Story Starters (Gr. 1-4) | EN75207 |
| Rewards 'n' Stuff (Gr. K-4) | EN75208 |

## REPRODUCIBLE ACTIVITY BOOKS

Here they are! Our fantastic instructional activity books with hundreds of effective applications. They fit right into your curriculum, provide valuable content for the student and motivate even the most reluctant learners.
- 48 pp — 8½" x 11" • Classroom tested and written by well-known teachers
- Curriculum-related objectives • Basic skills stressed • Pre and post tests
- Record sheets • Contemporary art themes • Awards • $3.95

**Math**
| | |
|---|---|
| Money Counts (Gr. 1-4) | EN73001 |
| Funtastic Calculator Math (Gr. 4-8) | EN73002 |
| Whole Numbers & Decimals (Gr. 4-8) | EN73007 |
| Mastering Fractions (Gr. 4-8) | EN73008 |
| Practical Metric Activities (Gr. 6 & up) | EN73010 |
| "Egg-Citing" Fractions (Gr. 3-6) | EN73011 |
| Centering on Math (Gr. K-3) | EN73015 |

**Reading/Language Arts**
| | |
|---|---|
| Look Sharp (Gr. K-3) | EN72001 |
| Alphabet Adventures (Gr. K-2) | EN72002 |
| Parade of Consonants (Gr. 1-3) | EN72003 |
| Parade of Vowels (Gr. 1-3) | EN72004 |
| Project Alphabetizing (Gr. 2-4) | EN72005 |
| Classy Calendar (Gr. K-3) | EN72006 |
| Write Now — Story Starters (Gr. 1-3) | EN72007 |
| Reading Projects (Gr. 2-4) | EN72008 |

## METRIC MATERIALS

Enrich also offers you the largest selection of effective metric teaching aids available. Partial listing shown below. Ask for a copy of our full color metric catalog containing over 100 measuring devices, books and kits for K-8.

| | |
|---|---|
| Measurement Book (Gr. K-3) $9.95 | EN44100 |
| Big Metric Resource Book (Gr. 3-8) $25.00 | EN41100 |
| Hometrics Book (Gr. 7 & up) $5.95 | EN43210 |
| Metric Posters (Gr. 6 & up) $4.00 | EN43220 |
| Cube-O-Grams and Activities $29.95 | EN84264 |

## POSTER ACTIVITY BOOKS

"Just what I've been looking for!" is what you'll say when you see these innovative, full color posters. Not only will they add charm to your classroom but they will offer you a wealth of ideas and activities. Use them to strengthen language development, creativity, independent thinking, problem solving and math concepts.

- Twelve 8½" x 11" FULL COLOR posters • Resource guide • Fun to use
- Individual or group participation • Appealing themes and art

**Math**
| | |
|---|---|
| Encountering Numbers (Gr. K-2) $4.95 (Ten 11" x 17" posters) | EN74003 |
| Fun With Super Shapes (Pre-School-2) $3.95 | EN74106 |
| Fun With Numbers (Pre-School-2) $3.95 | EN74107 |

**Reading/Language Arts**
| | |
|---|---|
| Robot Alphabets - Manuscript (Gr. K-2) $4.95 (28 posters) | EN74001 |
| Robot Alphabets - Cursive (Gr. 2-4) $4.95 (28 posters) | EN74002 |
| Fun With Colors (Pre-School-3) $3.95 | EN74101 |
| Creature Clues To Senses (Pre-School-3) $3.95 | EN74102 |
| Dinosaurs & Spatial Relationships (Pre-School-2) $3.95 | EN74103 |
| Cartoon Story Starters (Gr. 1-4) $3.95 | EN74104 |
| Super Classroom Helpers (Gr. 2-4) $3.95 | EN74105 |

## GAMEBOARD BOOKS

Take them to school and watch your students' faces light up! They fit into your curriculum and combine contemporary themes with basic skills.

- Five different FULL COLOR 11" x 16" Gameboards per book • Classroom tested • Teacher's guide • Self-contained complete with boards, and instructions — ready to go! • $4.95

**Math**
| | |
|---|---|
| Math Adventures + - × (Gr. 3-6) | EN73003 |
| Winning at Math - Div./Frac. (Gr. 4-8) | EN73004 |
| Perfecting Math Skills + - × (Gr. 3-6) | EN73005 |
| Plus & Minus Robots (Gr. 2-3) | EN73012 |
| Traveling Sums (Gr. 3-6) | EN73013 |

**Reading/Language Arts**
| | |
|---|---|
| Games to Motivate Learning (Gr. 3-8) | EN73006 |
| Word Computer (Gr. 4-6) | EN72015 |
| Creature Clues to Words (Gr. 4-6) | EN72016 |
| Spelling with Sports (Gr. 4-6) | EN72017 |
| Reference Book Adventures (Gr. 4-6) | EN72018 |

## READING CENTERS

Provides practical, relevant, high-interest themes that promote basic comprehensive skills and the student's natural interest in reading.

Here's a unique way to motivate interest in reading/language arts. This material provides practical, relevant, high-interest themes that promote basic comprehensive skills and the student's natural interest in reading.

- 6 FULL COLOR 11" x 16" boards in each • Unique Fun in Facts approach to reading comprehension • Teaches students to locate, interpret and extend facts • Improves vocabulary, creative thinking and writing • $4.95

| | |
|---|---|
| Great America (Gr. 5-8) | EN72009 |
| Marine World/Africa USA (Gr. 5-8) | EN72010 |
| Frontier Land (Gr. 5-8) | EN72011 |
| Yellow Pages (Gr. 5-8) | EN72012 |
| Using Menus (Gr. 5-8) | EN72013 |

**ENRICH** • 760 Kifer Road, Sunnyvale, CA 94086 • Printed in U.S.A. All rights reserved.